Write This Year

365 Daily Prompts to Build Your Writing Habit

hope✱writers

©2025 by Brian Dixon

Published by hope*books
2217 Matthews Township Pkwy
Suite D302
Matthews, NC 28105
www.hopebooks.com

hope*books is a division of hope*media

Printed in the United States of America

All rights reserved. Without limiting the rights under copyrights reserved above, no part of this publication may be scanned, uploaded, reproduced, distributed, or transmitted in any form or by any means whatsoever without express prior written permission from both the author and publisher of this book—except in the case of brief quotations embodied in critical articles and reviews.

Thank you for supporting the author's rights.

First edition.
Hardcover ISBN: 979-8-89185-408-6
Library of Congress Number: Application submitted; number pending

Welcome to *Write This Year*

This project has been a long time in the making. We started with daily writing prompts, and we quickly realized that one of the best things you can do as a writer ... is actually write.

For over 10 years, we've served writers at hope*writers, helping you discover, share, and publish your message of hope. The purpose of *Write This Year* is simple: give you a daily prompt and just enough space to start writing.

Some prompts will connect with you immediately and be easy to respond to. Others will challenge you to dig deeper and think more intentionally. That's the beauty of this tool—you can use it every day to develop a consistent writing practice, or you can open it when you're feeling stuck and need a spark.

At hope*writers, we teach the PAGES Framework—five types of writing that help you grow as a writer:

1. **Pause** – Write in your journal to process life.
2. **Align** – Reflect on your experiences and lessons learned.
3. **Grow** – Set your intentions and future goals.
4. **Encourage** – Write words that inspire and support others.
5. **Share** – Write words to publish, whether on a sticky note or in a book.

hope*writers

Write This Year can serve all five purposes. You might find some prompts that lead you to reflect on your life, others help you clarify your direction, and still others give you something you'll want to share publicly. How you use it is completely up to you.

Our hope is that this will be a resource you return to day after day, month after month, to help you write this year.

Happy writing!

Brian Dixon

CEO of hope*writers

How to Use the Monthly Reflection and Intention Sections

At the end of each month in *Write This Year*, you'll find a special space to **pause** and look back on your writing practice. This is your chance to notice what worked, what inspired you, and where you might want to make changes. It's not about judgment—it's about awareness and progress.

Then, at the start of each new month, you'll find a space to set **intentions** for the weeks ahead. This is where you decide, in advance, what you want your writing life to look and feel like.

Here's how each part works:

End-of-Month Reflection

This page is your opportunity to stop and take stock of your writing journey. Use it to measure your progress, celebrate your wins, and capture what you've learned—about writing and about yourself.

1. **How many days did you write this month?**

   Count the days you sat down to write, even if it was just for a few sentences. This isn't about perfection—it's about seeing your actual habits so you can build from there.

2. **How many times did you share your writing publicly?**

   Sharing means letting someone else read your work—in a social media post, an email, a blog, or even reading it aloud to a friend. Tracking this shows how often your words are making their way into the world.

3. **Which prompt felt the most inspiring this month?**

   Look back at the prompts you completed and notice the one that sparked the most energy for you. This will help you see what kinds of topics or questions bring out your best writing.

4. **On a scale of 1–10, how connected do you feel to your writing voice right now?**

   Your writing voice is the sound of *you* on the page—your style, your tone, your perspective. A "1" means you feel disconnected; a "10" means you feel strong and authentic. This number will change over time, and that's normal.

5. **What's one thing you learned about yourself through your writing this month?**

   Writing has a way of revealing things we didn't notice before—a hidden memory, a fresh perspective, or a new self-awareness. Capture at least one insight you gained this month.

New Month Intention

This section invites you to look ahead and choose how you want to approach the next month of writing. Being intentional now will help you stay motivated later.

1. **Word or theme for the month:** _____

   _____

Pick a single word or short phrase to guide your writing. It could be "consistent," "brave," "gratitude," or "explore." This becomes a touchstone you can return to when you need focus.

2. One skill I want to improve in my writing: _____

_____

Choose one specific skill to focus on. Maybe it's adding more details, telling more personal stories, editing after you write, or simply showing up more often. One focus keeps your growth manageable.

3. How many days will I commit to writing? _____

_____

Set a realistic number based on your current life and schedule. This isn't about aiming for perfection—it's about creating a goal you can actually reach.

4. One story or project I want to finish: _____

_____

Identify a specific piece of writing you want to complete this month—a blog post, a personal story, a chapter of your book, or even a letter you've been meaning to write.

5. I hope my writing this month will help me feel: _____

_____

Think about the emotional benefit you want from writing—peaceful, confident, joyful, focused. Linking your writing habit to how you want to feel can be a powerful motivator.

January

hope*writers

JANUARY 1

"In the beginning, God created ... and you can too. Today is the first blank page of your writing year."

Prompt:

Write down why you want to write this year. Be honest, even if it feels small.

January 2

"You don't have to write perfectly; you just have to write honestly."

Prompt:

Describe a moment from your life that still makes you smile.

January 3

"Small seeds grow into strong trees. Small words grow into strong stories."

Prompt:

Write about a small decision that changed the course of your life.

JANUARY 4

"Your story is a gift only you can give."

Prompt:

Write about a time someone encouraged you when you needed it most.

January 5

"The Lord is my shepherd; I lack nothing. In Him, you already have all you need to take the next step."

Prompt:

Write about a time you felt taken care of—by God or by someone else.

JANUARY 6

"The first step is rarely the hardest; it's deciding to take it."

Prompt:

Describe your first memory of writing something and how it made you feel.

JANUARY 7

"Stories connect hearts. Your words can build bridges."

Prompt:

Write about a person who changed your perspective.

JANUARY 8

"You can't edit a blank page. Write freely today."

Prompt:

Write about a day you wish you could relive—and why.

January 9

"God works through the ordinary. Your everyday life is worth writing about."

Prompt:

Describe your morning today in detail, as if you were telling a story.

January 10

"Even the shortest prayer is heard. Even the smallest story matters."

Prompt:

Write about a time you prayed and received an answer—big or small.

January 11

"Memories are treasures; words are the way we keep them."

Prompt:

Write about your favorite childhood place.

January 12

"Be still and listen—sometimes the story is already in your heart."

Prompt:

Write about a quiet moment you'll never forget.

January 13

"Courage is not the absence of fear; it's showing up anyway."

Prompt:

Write about a time you did something afraid.

January 14

"Light shines brightest in the dark. Your story can be that light for someone."

Prompt:

Write about a time you felt in the dark and what helped you through.

January 15

"The more you write, the easier it becomes to hear your own voice."

Prompt:

Describe your voice—not your physical voice, but your writing voice.

January 16

"Every day you write, you are building a habit that will serve you for life."

Prompt:

Write about a habit you're proud you've kept.

January 17

"God made you intentionally, for His glory—and that includes how you use your words."

Prompt:

Write about a time you knew you were exactly where you were meant to be.

January 18

"Your story doesn't have to be extraordinary to be meaningful."

Prompt:

Describe an ordinary day that meant more than you realized.

January 19

"The world needs your perspective—no one else has lived your exact story."

Prompt:

Write about something only you know how to do.

JANUARY 20

"Sometimes the story we need to write is the one we most need to hear."

Prompt:

Write a letter to your younger self.

January 21

"Your words can heal—both yourself and others."

Prompt:

Write about a time you forgave someone or were forgiven.

JANUARY 22

"Don't underestimate what God can do with your small, faithful words."

Prompt:
Write about a small act of kindness that made a big difference.

JANUARY 23

"Even Jesus told stories. Follow His example today."

Prompt:

Write a parable—a short story with a lesson.

January 24

"The story is already in you; your job is to let it out."

Prompt:

Write about a lesson life has taught you recently.

January 25

"Writing is a way to remember God's faithfulness."

Prompt:

Write about a time you felt God's presence in a hard season.

January 26

"Don't wait for the perfect time. Write now."

Prompt:

Describe your day so far as if it were the opening scene of a novel.

January 27

"Your future self will thank you for the words you write today."

Prompt:

Write a note to yourself to read one year from now.

JANUARY 28

"God's plan for your life includes the words you share."

Prompt:

Write about a dream God has placed in your heart.

JANUARY 29

"A story becomes more powerful the more it is shared."

Prompt:

Write about a family story you've heard more than once.

January 30

"Progress, not perfection, is the goal."

Prompt:

Write about a time you learned something by making a mistake.

hope*writers

JANUARY 31

"You've just completed your first month—imagine what the rest of the year holds."

Prompt:

Write about how you feel after 31 days of writing.

January – New Beginnings

End-of-Month Reflection

- How many days did you write this month?
- How many times did you share your writing publicly?
- Which prompt felt the most inspiring to start your year?
- On a scale of 1–10, how connected do you feel to your writing voice right now?
- What's one thing you learned about yourself through your writing this month?

New Month Intention (*February*)

- Word or theme for the next month: _____
- One skill I want to improve in my writing: _____
- How many days will I commit to writing? _____
- One story or project I want to finish: _____
- I hope my writing this month will help me feel: _____

February

hope*writers

FEBRUARY 1

"God makes all things new—including your writing life."

Prompt:

Think about a time in the past two years when you felt like you got a fresh start—maybe moving to a new place, beginning a new job, or starting a new habit. Describe where you were, what was happening, and what you were hoping for.

February 2

"You don't have to tell the whole story at once. Just start with one scene."

Prompt:

Choose one moment from the last week (a conversation, a meal, a walk outside). Write it out as if it's the opening scene of a short story, including what you saw, heard, and felt.

FEBRUARY 3

"Your words can be a shelter for someone else's heart."

Prompt:

Think of someone in your life who's going through a hard time. Write a short letter to them, telling a personal story from your life that might give them comfort.

FEBRUARY 4

"Faith is taking the first step without seeing the whole staircase."

Prompt:

Describe a time when you said "yes" to something without knowing how it would turn out. Include what you were afraid of, what you prayed about, and what happened next.

FEBRUARY 5

"Sometimes the smallest details tell the biggest truths."

Prompt:

Describe your favorite meal in full detail—where you were when you last had it, what the plate looked like, the smell in the air, and the first bite.

FEBRUARY 6

"The people in your life are part of your story."

Prompt:

Write about a teacher, pastor, coach, or mentor who shaped who you are. Tell one specific memory of something they said or did that stayed with you.

FEBRUARY 7

"God's fingerprints are on your past, present, and future."

Prompt:

Write about a time when you felt "in the right place at the right time." Include the small details that made you realize God was guiding you.

February 8

"When you feel stuck, remember—even a sentence is progress."

Prompt:

Write one sentence about how you feel right now. Then, expand it into a paragraph by adding what happened today to make you feel that way.

hope*writers

FEBRUARY 9

"Your story is a living testimony."

Prompt:

Think of a prayer you once prayed that didn't get answered right away, but later, you could see why. Write the before, the waiting, and the after.

FEBRUARY 10

"Some stories are for the world. Some are just for you and God."

Prompt:

Write about a private moment you shared with God, maybe during a walk, in prayer, or while reading Scripture. Describe the setting and the emotion.

February 11

"Love is patient, love is kind ... and love is worth writing about."

Prompt:

Describe a time someone showed you love without saying a word through an action, a gesture, or simply their presence.

FEBRUARY 12

"Your past doesn't define you—but it can inspire others."

Prompt:

Write about a time you failed or made a mistake. Include how you felt in the moment and what you learned looking back.

February 13

"Gratitude changes the way we see our own story."

Prompt:

Make a quick list of 10 things you're thankful for right now. Choose one and write about the last time you experienced it.

February 14

"We love because He first loved us."

Prompt:

Write about a time you felt deeply loved by God through an answered prayer, a moment of peace, or an unexpected blessing.

February 15

"Every chapter has a purpose—even the hard ones."

Prompt:

Think of a difficult season in your life. Write about one person, place, or event from that time that helped you make it through.

FEBRUARY 16

"Joy can be found in the simplest moments."

Prompt:

Describe a small joy from the past week: a laugh, a good meal, a conversation. Write it like you're telling it to a friend who wasn't there.

February 17

"Your words may be the encouragement someone needs today."

Prompt:

Write a note to a younger version of yourself — choose an age where you needed encouragement — and tell yourself what you wish you'd known then.

FEBRUARY 18

"When God calls you to a work—whether in ministry, service, or writing—He provides the grace and strength to do it."

Prompt:

Write about a time you had to do something you felt unqualified for. Share how you prepared (or didn't), how it turned out, and what you learned.

February 19

"Some stories begin with a question."

Prompt:

Write about a question you've carried for years. Describe the moments in life that have made it louder or quieter.

FEBRUARY 20

"Hope grows when it's shared."

Prompt:

Write about a time someone gave you hope when you didn't have much. Then write about how you've passed that hope on to someone else.

February 21

"You are living a story worth telling."

Prompt:

Pretend you're meeting someone for the first time. Write the story you'd tell them about who you are and where you've come from.

FEBRUARY 22

"God can use your ordinary to do something extraordinary."

Prompt:

Write about a normal day that unexpectedly turned into something special: a phone call, a surprise visitor, a moment you didn't see coming.

FEBRUARY 23

"Even when you don't know what to write, you can write what you know."

Prompt:

Describe your favorite place in as much sensory detail as you can (sights, sounds, smells, and feelings).

FEBRUARY 24

"Some stories are written in ink, others on hearts."

Prompt:

Write about a person whose influence still shapes your decisions today. Tell one specific story that shows why.

hope*writers

FEBRUARY 25

"God can turn your test into a testimony."

Prompt:

Write about a time you went through a trial and came out stronger. Describe the before, the struggle, and the breakthrough.

FEBRUARY 26

"A single word can change a life. Choose them wisely."

Prompt:

Write about a word or phrase that has stuck with you for years—who said it, where you were, and why it mattered.

February 27

"Your story is part of a bigger story—God's story."

Prompt:

Write about a time when you could clearly see God weaving together events for a purpose.

FEBRUARY 28

"You've made it through two months—keep going."

Prompt:

Write about the biggest change you've noticed in yourself since you began writing daily. Include an example of a specific day or moment that shows it.

FEBRUARY – FINDING YOUR RHYTHM

End-of-Month Reflection

- How many days did you write this month?
- Did you begin to find a consistent time or place to write?
- Which prompt challenged you the most? Why?
- How often did writing help you process emotions this month?
- Did any writing surprise you by revealing something new?

New Month Intention *(March)*

- Word or theme for the next month: _____
- My primary writing goal: _____
- How many days will I commit to writing? _____
- One relationship I want to write about or for: _____
- I hope my writing this month will encourage: _____

March

hope*writers

hope*writers

MARCH 1

"Every month is a fresh page. Start today with bold words."

Prompt:

Write about a risk you've taken—big or small. Describe what happened before, during, and after, and how it shaped you.

March 2

"God often speaks through the people He places in our path."

Prompt:

Think of a conversation that changed your thinking. Write out the dialogue as best as you remember it.

March 3

"Your life is made of moments—write one down before it slips away."

Prompt:

Describe one moment from yesterday in as much sensory detail as possible: sights, smells, sounds, and feelings.

March 4

"Faith looks forward—even when the road isn't clear."

Prompt:

Write about a time you stepped into something new not knowing what would happen. What did you learn about God in the process?

March 5

"Sometimes the quiet speaks the loudest."

Prompt:

Describe a moment of stillness you've experienced, maybe during prayer, on a walk, or in nature. What thoughts or feelings came up?

MARCH 6

"You can find God's fingerprints in your past if you look closely."

Prompt:

Think of a hard season in your life. Write about one way you now see God was at work in that time.

hope*writers

March 7

"Your unique perspective is part of the gift God gave you."

Prompt:

Write about a place you know well (your kitchen, a park, your church) as if you were describing it to someone who's never been there.

MARCH 8

"Small beginnings can lead to big change."

Prompt:

Write about the first step you took toward something important in your life. Describe what made you take it.

March 9

"God can use even your ordinary days for His glory."

Prompt:

Write about a day that started out ordinary but turned into something unforgettable.

MARCH 10

"Your scars can be someone else's sign of hope."

Prompt:

Write about a wound (physical or emotional) and how it healed over time.

March 11

"The details you notice can make your writing come alive."

Prompt:

Pick an everyday object near you: a mug, a chair, a Bible. Describe it in vivid detail without naming it directly.

MARCH 12

"God calls us to remember His faithfulness."

Prompt:

Write about a specific answered prayer. Include the waiting period and the moment you realized it had been answered.

March 13

"Even a short story can hold deep truth."

Prompt:

Write about a single act of kindness you've received. Keep it under 200 words.

March 14

"Your voice matters, even if you feel small."

Prompt:

Describe a time you spoke up for something you believed in—and what happened next.

March 15

"God can redeem every chapter."

Prompt:

Write about something from your past you once wished you could erase, and how God has used it for good.

MARCH 16

"The way you tell a story can make it unforgettable."

Prompt:

Take a funny memory and write it as if it were a suspenseful story. Then, in a second paragraph, tell it as comedy.

hope*writers

MARCH 17

"God delights in your joy."

Prompt:

Write about a celebration in your life—a birthday, holiday, or personal milestone. Describe the sights, sounds, and emotions.

MARCH 18

"You never know who needs to hear your story."

Prompt:

Write a story from your life that you'd want to tell your younger self.

MARCH 19

"Every person you meet is a story in progress."

Prompt:

Write about a stranger who caught your attention on a trip, at a coffee shop, or in passing. Imagine their story.

MARCH 20

"Spring is proof that God brings new life."

Prompt:

Describe the first signs of spring where you live (colors, smells, sounds) and how they make you feel.

MARCH 21

"God uses both the mountaintops and the valleys."

Prompt:

Write about one high point and one low point from the past year. What do they have in common?

MARCH 22

"Your story can inspire someone you'll never meet."

Prompt:

Write about a time you read or heard a story that encouraged you. How did it change you?

hope✳writers

MARCH 23

"God is with you in every season."

Prompt:

Write about a moment when you felt God's presence unexpectedly—maybe in a place you didn't think you'd find Him.

MARCH 24

"The best stories often start with a single memory."

Prompt:

Write about your earliest memory. Include where you were, who was there, and how it made you feel.

March 25

"God cares about the desires of your heart."

Prompt:

Write about something you wanted for a long time and finally received.

MARCH 26

"Writing helps you see your life through God's lens."

Prompt:

Pick a difficult event in your life and retell it from the perspective of someone who loves you.

March 27

"You don't have to have it all figured out to start."

Prompt:

Write about something you began without having all the answers. How did it turn out?

MARCH 28

"God can use even the smallest acts for great impact."

Prompt:

Write about a time you did something that seemed small but had a big effect on someone else.

MARCH 29

"Sometimes you need to write it before you can speak it."

Prompt:

Write out a conversation you've been wanting to have with someone.

MARCH 30

"God's plans are better than ours."

Prompt:

Write about a time when things didn't go your way but ended up better than expected.

MARCH 31

"You've written for three months. God is building something in you."

Prompt:

Look back at your January 1 entry. Write about what's changed in your perspective since then.

March – Growth Mindset

End-of-Month Reflection

- How many days did you write this month?
- Did you try any new writing styles or formats?
- What was your proudest piece this month?
- Which day's prompt helped you think in a new way?
- How confident do you feel in your writing voice right now (1–10)?

New Month Intention *(April)*

- Word or theme for the next month: _____
- One new writing experiment I want to try: _____
- How many days will I commit to writing? _____
- I want my writing this month to grow in: _____
- I hope my writing this month will inspire: _____

April

hope*writers

April 1

"God writes the best plot twists."

Prompt:

Write about a time something turned out completely differently than you expected, for better or worse. Include the moment you realized the change.

APRIL 2

"Your life holds stories no one else can tell."

Prompt:

Write about a family tradition you grew up with. Describe the setting, people, and any unique details that made it special.

APRIL 3

"Even the smallest memory can hold great meaning."

Prompt:

Describe a smell that takes you back to a specific moment in time. Tell the story connected to that smell.

April 4

"God is present in both the storms and the sunshine."

Prompt:

Write about a literal storm you've experienced—a thunderstorm, blizzard, or hurricane—and how it made you feel.

April 5

"Your perspective can bring comfort to someone else."

Prompt:

Write a short letter to a friend who's going through a hard time, sharing a story from your own life that offers hope.

April 6

"God's timing is perfect, even when it feels slow."

Prompt:

Write about something you had to wait for and how that waiting shaped you.

hope✻writers

APRIL 7

"Your surroundings can inspire your story."

Prompt:

Describe the view from your window right now. Include as many details as possible: colors, movement, light, shadows.

April 8

"God often answers prayers in unexpected ways."

Prompt:

Write about a time you prayed for something specific but got an answer you didn't expect.

April 9

"The smallest act of kindness can leave a lasting mark."

Prompt:

Write about a time a stranger was unexpectedly kind to you. Describe where you were and how it made you feel.

April 10

"Your ordinary days are worth writing about."

Prompt:

Walk through your morning routine step by step as if you were describing it to someone from another country who has never experienced it.

APRIL 11

"God calls us to remember His works."

Prompt:

Write about a time you clearly saw God working in your life—and how you knew it was Him.

April 12

"Your story matters because it's part of God's story."

Prompt:

Write about a time you were part of something bigger than yourself (a group project, mission trip, or event).

April 13

"The details make the memory come alive."

Prompt:

Describe a favorite outfit you've worn—where you got it, when you wore it, and why you loved it.

APRIL 14

"God uses the people in our lives to shape us."

Prompt:

Write about a friendship that has lasted for years. Tell the story of how you met.

April 15

"Your story might be the answer to someone else's prayer."

Prompt:

Write about a time you shared something personal and it encouraged another person.

April 16

"God meets us in the places we least expect."

Prompt:

Describe a moment when you felt God's presence in an unlikely place: maybe in a car, at the grocery store, or on a walk.

April 17

"Some lessons take time to understand."

Prompt:

Write about a piece of advice you didn't understand when you first heard it but now makes sense.

APRIL 18

"Your memories are a treasure chest waiting to be opened."

Prompt:

Write about a specific childhood birthday. Include where you were, who was there, and what made it memorable.

hope*writers

APRIL 19

"God's faithfulness is worth recording."

Prompt:

Write about a time when God provided for you in a surprising way.

April 20

"The beauty of creation tells God's story too."

Prompt:

Describe a place in nature that makes you feel peaceful. Capture every sight, sound, and smell.

April 21

"Your story has room for both joy and sorrow."

Prompt:

Write about a time when you laughed and cried on the same day.

April 22

"God can use the simplest moments to speak to us."

Prompt:

Write about a time something small (a phrase, a song, a Bible verse) gave you exactly what you needed that day.

April 23

"Your writing can help you see God's hand in your life."

Prompt:

Pick a challenging season and write about it from the perspective of gratitude.

April 24

"God often teaches us through change."

Prompt:

Write about a big change you've gone through (a move, a new role, a transition) and what it taught you.

April 25

"The people who love you are part of your testimony."

Prompt:

Write about a time you felt truly supported by someone. Describe the moment in detail.

April 26

"God's grace meets you right where you are."

Prompt:

Write about a mistake you made and how you experienced grace afterward.

hope*writers

APRIL 27

"Your story can preserve memories for the next generation."

Prompt:

Write about a family member you wish more people could know. Share one specific memory with them.

April 28

"Even small beginnings can have a big impact."

Prompt:

Write about a time you started something small that grew into more than you expected.

APRIL 29

"God's plan is always better than our plan."

Prompt:

Write about a time your original plan fell apart and what ended up happening instead.

April 30

"You've written for four months—your words are adding up."

Prompt:

Write about what has surprised you most about daily writing so far.

APRIL – FRESH PERSPECTIVE

End-of-Month Reflection

- How many days did you write this month?
- What part of your writing process feels easier than it did in January?
- Which prompt brought up a memory you hadn't thought about in years?
- Did you notice any patterns or themes in your writing?
- How would you describe your writing energy this month?

New Month Intention *(May)*

- Word or theme for the next month: _____
- One topic I want to explore deeper: _____
- How many days will I commit to writing? _____
- One way I want to share my writing: _____
- I hope my writing this month will help me see: _____
-

May

hope*writers

MAY 1

"God makes beauty out of the broken pieces."

Prompt:

Write about a time when something you thought was ruined turned into something good. Include the moment your perspective began to change.

May 2

"Your story can shine light into someone else's darkness."

Prompt:

Think of a time you were in a dark or difficult season. Write about what helped you keep going.

May 3

"God often speaks through the voices of others."

Prompt:

Write about a piece of advice someone gave you that stayed with you. Describe when you heard it and why it mattered.

MAY 4

"The ordinary moments are worth remembering."

Prompt:

Describe what a typical Sunday looks like for you right now. Capture the sounds, sights, and feelings of the day.

hope*writers

May 5

"God's creation is full of reminders of His care."

Prompt:

Write about a time you noticed something beautiful in nature and felt it was meant just for you.

May 6

"Your words can be a gift to the people you love."

Prompt:

Write a letter to someone in your family telling them one thing you admire about them, with a specific example.

May 7

"God works in both the waiting and the moving."

Prompt:

Write about a time you were eager to move forward but God seemed to say, "Wait." What happened in that waiting season?

May 8

"Your memories are part of God's faithfulness."

Prompt:

Describe a favorite memory from school (a teacher, a field trip, or a moment with friends).

May 9

"God can use your pain to help someone else heal."

Prompt:

Write about a painful experience that you've since shared with someone else—and how it helped them.

MAY 10

"Sometimes joy comes in the smallest packages."

Prompt:

Write about a small gift you've received—not just physical, but also a compliment, gesture, or moment of laughter.

May 11

"God's story is woven into yours."

Prompt:

Write about a specific time you felt God guiding your steps, even in little decisions.

May 12

"Your story matters to the people who come after you."

Prompt:

Write about something you hope your children or grandchildren will know about your life.

May 13

"God can use your voice in unexpected ways."

Prompt:

Write about a time you spoke up for something important, even if it felt uncomfortable.

MAY 14

"Gratitude changes how we see the world."

Prompt:

Write about a time you intentionally chose gratitude, even though you didn't feel like it.

May 15

"Your relationships are part of your testimony."

Prompt:

Write about a friendship that ended. Include what you learned from it.

May 16

"God's timing is never too late."

Prompt:

Write about something you thought would never happen, but it did, and it was worth the wait.

MAY 17

"Your words can breathe life into someone else's dream."

Prompt:

Write about a time someone encouraged you to pursue a goal. Describe exactly what they said.

May 18

"God uses both successes and failures to shape us."

Prompt:

Write about a time you failed but learned something that helped you later.

May 19

"Every person in your life is a potential story."

Prompt:

Write about a neighbor you've had. Describe what made them memorable.

MAY 20

"God's fingerprints are in the details."

Prompt:

Describe an ordinary object in your home that holds a meaningful story.

MAY 21

"Your story is a work in progress—and that's okay."

Prompt:

Write about something in your life that's still unfinished. How do you feel about it?

MAY 22

"God can use one small moment to change everything."

Prompt:

Write about a five-minute period in your life that changed you forever.

MAY 23

"Even the valleys have value."

Prompt:

Write about a time you felt far from God. What helped you find your way back?

May 24

"Your unique view of the world is worth sharing."

Prompt:

Write about a place you've traveled to—near or far—and how it looked, smelled, and felt.

MAY 25

"God uses your past to prepare you for your future."

Prompt:

Write about a skill you learned long ago that you still use today.

MAY 26

"Some of God's lessons come through laughter."

Prompt:

Write about a funny moment that happened at church, with family, or among friends.

May 27

"God can meet you anywhere."

Prompt:

Write about a time you felt God's presence in a surprising location.

May 28

"Even the smallest habit can make a big difference."

Prompt:

Write about a daily habit that helps you feel closer to God.

hope*writers

MAY 29

"Your story can inspire courage in others."

Prompt:

Write about a time you took a leap of faith and what happened as a result.

May 30

"God's goodness is worth remembering."

Prompt:

Write about a time you received an unexpected blessing.

May 31

"You've written for five months—and you're building something that lasts."

Prompt:

Write about the biggest benefit you've noticed from writing regularly.

May – Building Momentum

End-of-Month Reflection

- How many days did you write this month?
- How has your consistency improved?
- Which prompt was the easiest to write this month?
- Which prompt pushed you the most?
- Has your confidence in your storytelling grown? How?

New Month Intention *(June)*

- Word or theme for the next month: _____
- One writing habit I want to strengthen: _____
- How many days will I commit to writing? _____
- A story from my life I want to capture: _____
- I hope my writing this month will remind me of: _____

June

hope*writers

June 1

"God is doing a new thing—can you see it?"

Prompt:

Write about a new opportunity, habit, or relationship in your life right now. Describe what excites you about it and what makes you nervous.

JUNE 2

"Your story can plant seeds in someone else's heart."

Prompt:

Write about a time someone told you a story that stayed with you for years. Explain why it stuck.

June 3

"God uses even the smallest details to remind us of His care."

Prompt:

Describe an object you keep for sentimental reasons. Tell the story of how you got it and why you've kept it.

JUNE 4

"Your pain can become someone else's lifeline."

Prompt:

Write about a season of struggle and one piece of wisdom you gained from it.

June 5

"Every day is a page in your story."

Prompt:

Write about everything that happened in the last 24 hours as if you were narrating a chapter in a memoir.

JUNE 6

"God works through the people He places in our lives."

Prompt:

Write about a person you've met in the past year who's had a positive influence on you. Share the first time you met them.

June 7

"Even ordinary places can hold extraordinary meaning."

Prompt:

Describe a place you've visited countless times—like a favorite coffee shop, a park, or a room in your home—and what it means to you.

June 8

"God's timing often looks different from ours."

Prompt:

Write about something you prayed for that took longer than you hoped. Describe what you learned in the waiting.

JUNE 9

"Your perspective can change how the story ends."

Prompt:

Take a difficult event in your life and rewrite it from a hopeful point of view.

JUNE 10

"Small moments can reveal big truths."

Prompt:

Describe a single conversation or comment that shifted the way you saw a situation.

JUNE 11

"God meets you in the quiet."

Prompt:

Write about a time when being alone brought you peace rather than loneliness.

JUNE 12

"Your story might be the answer to someone's prayer."

Prompt:

Write about a time you shared your experience and later learned it helped someone.

hope✷writers

JUNE 13

"God uses every chapter—even the messy ones."

Prompt:

Write about a time you felt like you were failing but later realized you were growing.

June 14

"Memories are the threads of your story."

Prompt:

Describe a summer memory from childhood. Include what you saw, heard, and felt.

June 15

"Your words can encourage someone to keep going."

Prompt:

Write a short note of encouragement to someone you know who's working toward a big goal.

June 16

"God is faithful in every season."

Prompt:

Write about a time you were worried about the future but later saw God's provision.

JUNE 17

"The little things are often the big things."

Prompt:

Describe a simple pleasure in your daily life (your morning coffee, a favorite walk, or a pet) and why it matters to you.

JUNE 18

"God can use your past to prepare you for your calling."

Prompt:

Write about a skill or talent you developed years ago that's still serving you today.

JUNE 19

"Your story is a reflection of God's grace."

Prompt:

Write about a time you made a mistake but were shown grace instead of judgment.

JUNE 20

"God's creation can speak to our hearts."

Prompt:

Describe your favorite type of weather and the feelings or memories it brings.

hope✻writers

JUNE 21

"Your story is worth telling while you're living it."

Prompt:

Write about something that happened today that future-you might want to remember.

JUNE 22

"God often works behind the scenes."

Prompt:

Write about a time when you didn't see God's hand until later.

JUNE 23

"The people you meet can shape the chapters you write."

Prompt:

Write about a person who came into your life for a short season but left a lasting impact.

June 24

"God's goodness can be seen in the details."

Prompt:

Describe your favorite meal in such detail that the reader can smell and taste it.

JUNE 25

"Your testimony is powerful, even in small pieces."

Prompt:

Write about a time you told someone part of your story and saw it encourage them.

JUNE 26

"God often answers prayers in ways we don't expect."

Prompt:

Write about a time you received something different from what you prayed for and why it turned out to be better.

hope*writers

JUNE 27

"The hard days can produce the deepest faith."

Prompt:

Write about one particularly hard day and how you made it through.

JUNE 28

"God can bring joy in the middle of difficulty."

Prompt:

Write about a time you laughed during a season when life was hard.

hope*writers

JUNE 29

"Your life is filled with stories worth telling."

Prompt:

Write about a random memory that popped into your head recently. Explore why you think you remembered it.

JUNE 30

"You've completed six months of daily writing—keep building the habit."

Prompt:

Write about the biggest personal change you've noticed since starting this journey.

JUNE – MID-YEAR CHECK-IN

End-of-Month Reflection

- How many days did you write this month?
- At the halfway point of the year, what progress are you most proud of?
- Which prompt gave you the biggest emotional breakthrough?
- How has writing impacted your faith or outlook so far?
- What's one thing you want to improve in the second half of the year?

New Month Intention *(July)*

- Word or theme for the next month: _____
- One story I want to tell before summer ends: _____
- How many days will I commit to writing? _____
- One audience I'd like to share my words with: _____
- I hope my writing this month will give me: _____

July

hope*writers

JULY 1

"God's mercies are new every morning—and every month."

Prompt:

Write about one thing you want to focus on this month and why it matters to you.

July 2

"Your story is shaped by the people you meet."

Prompt:

Write about a time a stranger's kindness surprised you. Describe exactly what they did and how you felt.

July 3

"God is in the details—even the ones you almost miss."

Prompt:

Describe a small detail you noticed today that made you smile.

July 4

"Freedom is worth celebrating."

Prompt:

Write about a time you experienced freedom in your faith, your relationships, or your personal life.

July 5

"God can bring beauty out of the unexpected."

Prompt:

Write about a plan that didn't work out but led to something better.

JULY 6

"Your story can strengthen someone's faith."

Prompt:

Write about a time when God answered a prayer in a way that built your trust in Him.

July 7

"Every person carries a story worth hearing."

Prompt:

Write about someone you've known for years but recently learned something new about.

July 8

"God often works through the simplest moments."

Prompt:
Write about a simple, everyday routine you love.

July 9

"Your past can guide your future."

Prompt:

Write about a lesson you learned the hard way and how it shapes your decisions now.

JULY 10

"God's creation reflects His beauty."

Prompt:

Describe a sunset, sunrise, or night sky you've seen and what it made you think about.

JULY 11

"Your words can help someone feel less alone."

Prompt:

Write about a time when someone's story made you feel understood.

JULY 12

"God can use your weaknesses for His glory."

Prompt:

Write about something you've struggled with that ended up becoming a strength.

July 13

"Even a small step forward is still progress."

Prompt:

Write about a goal you've been working toward, even if it's going slowly.

July 14

"Life has a way of surprising us when we're not looking for it."

Prompt:

Write about a time you felt God's presence in an unusual place.

July 15

"Your story might be exactly what someone needs today."

Prompt:

Write about a time you shared something personal and saw it encourage another person.

July 16

"God can use the unexpected to grow your faith."

Prompt:

Write about a time when an interruption led to something good.

July 17

"Your memories are part of your legacy."

Prompt:

Write about a story you hope will be told about you someday.

July 18

"God's timing is always perfect."

Prompt:

Write about a time when you realized later that the timing of something was just right.

July 19

"Your perspective matters."

Prompt:

Pick a memory and write about it from someone else's point of view.

July 20

"God is with you in both the ordinary and the extraordinary."

Prompt:

Write about a normal day in your life right now that you think you'll remember years from now.

JULY 21

"Your words can bring healing."

Prompt:

Write a letter of encouragement to someone going through a hard time.

July 22

"God is present even in the waiting."

Prompt:

Write about a time you were waiting for an answer and what you did during that season.

JULY 23

"Your story can inspire hope."

Prompt:

Write about a time you overcame fear and did something anyway.

July 24

"God often speaks in whispers, not shouts."

Prompt:
Write about a time when you felt a quiet nudge to take action.

July 25

"Your relationships are a gift from God."

Prompt:

Write about a friendship that has encouraged your faith.

July 26

"God can bring joy even in difficult seasons."

Prompt:

Write about a moment of laughter in the middle of a hard time.

July 27

"Your story can show others what's possible."

Prompt:

Write about something you once thought you couldn't do—but did.

JULY 28

"God's fingerprints are everywhere."

Prompt:

Describe a time when you recognized God's hand in your circumstances.

July 29

"Your words can create connection."

Prompt:

Write about a conversation you had that brought you closer to someone.

July 30

"God's plans are greater than our own."

Prompt:

Write about a time when you were thankful something didn't go the way you planned.

hope✳writers

JULY 31

"You've completed seven months of writing. Keep building the story God's given you."

Prompt:

Write about one theme you've noticed appearing in your writing so far this year.

July – Deepening Your Voice

End-of-Month Reflection

- How many days did you write this month?
- Which prompt helped you write with more honesty?
- What's one topic you want to keep exploring?
- Have you noticed growth in how you describe details?
- How comfortable are you sharing your words publicly right now (1–10)?

New Month Intention *(August)*

- Word or theme for the next month: _____
- One truth I want to express more boldly: _____
- How many days will I commit to writing? _____
- One way I'll take a risk with my writing: _____
- I hope my writing this month will connect me with: _____

August

hope*writers

AUGUST 1

"God's mercies are new every morning—and so are your opportunities to write."

Prompt:

Write about one thing you're looking forward to this month and why it excites you.

AUGUST 2

"Your story may be the answer to someone's silent prayer."

Prompt:

Write about a time you shared an experience and later learned it gave someone hope.

AUGUST 3

"God works through both the expected and the unexpected."

Prompt:

Write about a plan that went exactly as you hoped and how that felt.

AUGUST 4

"The details make your story come alive."

Prompt:

Describe your favorite meal from start to finish. Include the smell, taste, sounds, and setting.

AUGUST 5

"God uses people to show His love."

Prompt:

Write about a time a friend or family member helped you when you needed it most.

August 6

"Even the smallest habit can change your life."

Prompt:

Write about a habit you've built that has made a difference for you.

August 7

"God is with you in both the highs and the lows."

Prompt:

Write about one of your happiest memories and one of your hardest—and what connects them.

August 8

"Your story can help someone else keep going."

Prompt:

Write about a challenge you overcame and one practical thing that helped you through it.

AUGUST 9

"God can meet you in the ordinary."

Prompt:

Describe a simple moment from today that made you pause and be thankful.

AUGUST 10

"Your words can change the way someone sees themselves."

Prompt:
Write about a time someone said something kind to you that you've never forgotten.

August 11

"Delays can turn into opportunities we didn't see at first."

Prompt:

Think of a time you didn't get what you wanted right away — what did the delay teach you?

AUGUST 12

"Your memories are worth preserving."

Prompt:

Write about a favorite summer memory from childhood.

AUGUST 13

"God can turn obstacles into opportunities."

Prompt:

Write about a time a problem led you to a creative solution.

AUGUST 14

"Your relationships are part of God's plan for your life."

Prompt:

Write about a person you met by chance who became important to you.

AUGUST 15

"God often speaks in stillness."

Prompt:

Write about a quiet moment when you felt God's presence clearly.

AUGUST 16

"Your story can inspire someone to take the next step."

Prompt:

Write about a time you encouraged someone to try something new and what happened.

AUGUST 17

"The world outside often reminds us to slow down."

Prompt:

Describe a natural place that clears your head when life feels heavy.

August 18

"Honest words can help repair trust."

Prompt:

Write about a time you apologized to someone—or they apologized to you—and what changed afterward.

AUGUST 19

"God uses every chapter of your life for a purpose."

Prompt:

Write about a season that felt wasted but turned out to be meaningful.

AUGUST 20

"Your life holds lessons worth sharing."

Prompt:

Write about something you've learned in the past year that you wish you had known sooner.

AUGUST 21

"God can turn small beginnings into great stories."

Prompt:

Write about the first step you took toward a goal and how it felt.

AUGUST 22

"Your story is part of something bigger."

Prompt:

Write about a time you were part of a group, team, or church project that made a difference.

AUGUST 23

"God's blessings can come in disguise."

Prompt:

Write about something that felt like a setback at first but turned out to be a blessing.

AUGUST 24

"Your memories are treasures to pass down."

Prompt:

Write about an object you've kept because of the memory attached to it.

August 25

"God can use your words to speak truth."

Prompt:

Write about a time you had to be honest with someone, even when it was hard.

August 26

"Your story can remind others they're not alone."

Prompt:

Write about a time you realized someone else had gone through the same thing you were experiencing.

August 27

"God can meet you in your weakness."

Prompt:

Write about a time you felt inadequate but found the strength to move forward.

AUGUST 28

"Your words can celebrate God's goodness."

Prompt:

Write about a recent moment that filled you with gratitude.

AUGUST 29

"God often uses interruptions for His purposes."

Prompt:

Write about a time your day was interrupted and something good came from it.

AUGUST 30

"Your story is still being written."

Prompt:

Write about an area of your life where you're still waiting to see how it turns out.

AUGUST 31

"You've completed eight months. Your daily faithfulness is building something beautiful."

Prompt:

Write about how your approach to writing has changed since January 1.

August – Expanding Horizons

End-of-Month Reflection

- How many days did you write this month?
- Did you write about anything unexpected?
- Which prompt stretched your creativity the most?
- What's one thing you learned about yourself this month?
- How did your writing impact your relationships?

New Month Intention *(September)*

- Word or theme for the next month: _____
- One new topic I want to explore: _____
- How many days will I commit to writing? _____
- One way I want to use my writing to serve others: _____
- I hope my writing this month will help me understand: _____

September

hope*writers

SEPTEMBER 1

"God's mercies don't run out at the start of a new month."

Prompt:

Write about one thing you want to focus on this month and how you plan to make it happen.

SEPTEMBER 2

"Your story can bring peace to someone else's storm."

Prompt:

Write about a time you encouraged someone who was struggling: what you said and how they responded.

September 3

"God works in the details others might overlook."

Prompt:

Describe a small detail from your day that reminded you of God's presence.

SEPTEMBER 4

"Even the hardest seasons can bring wisdom."

Prompt:

Write about a difficult time and the single most important lesson you learned from it.

September 5

"God often uses people to show His love."

Prompt:

Write about someone who prayed for you or supported you in a specific way.

SEPTEMBER 6

"Your words have the power to encourage."

Prompt:

Write a short note of encouragement to someone you know is facing a challenge.

SEPTEMBER 7

"God's timing is worth trusting."

Prompt:

Write about something you wanted to happen quickly but took longer—and why the delay was a gift.

SEPTEMBER 8

"Your story is part of God's bigger picture."

Prompt:

Write about a time you realized your actions or choices affected more people than you expected.

SEPTEMBER 9

"Daily routines can offer comfort and clarity."

Prompt:

Describe a simple part of your daily routine that helps you feel close to God.

SEPTEMBER 10

"Supportive relationships give strength in every season."

Prompt:

Write about a friend or family member who has been a steady source of support.

SEPTEMBER 11

"God can bring light in the darkest moments."

Prompt:

Write about a time you were afraid and how you found courage.

SEPTEMBER 12

"Your story might be the hope someone else needs."

Prompt:

Write about a time you shared your testimony and saw it impact someone.

September 13

"God's creation speaks of His greatness."

Prompt:

Describe a time you were in awe of nature and how it made you feel.

SEPTEMBER 14

"Even small beginnings can grow into great things."

Prompt:

Write about something you started small and watched grow—a relationship, a habit, or a project.

SEPTEMBER 15

"God uses people to shape our stories."

Prompt:

Write about a mentor, teacher, or pastor who influenced your life and one specific lesson they taught you.

SEPTEMBER 16

"A single exchange can change the way we see each other."

Prompt:

Write about a conversation that deepened a relationship.

September 17

"The highs and lows of the year both shape who we are."

Prompt:

Write about a moment this past year that gave you a sense of direction.

September 18

"Your perspective can change a situation."

Prompt:

Write about a time you chose to see something differently and how it changed the outcome.

SEPTEMBER 19

"God's blessings often come through people."

Prompt:

Write about a time someone showed you generosity.

SEPTEMBER 20

"Your life holds stories worth remembering."

Prompt:

Write about a story from your childhood that you've told more than once.

SEPTEMBER 21

"God's grace can meet you in your failures."

Prompt:

Write about a mistake you made and what you learned from it.

SEPTEMBER 22

"Your story is still unfolding."

Prompt:

Write about a dream you're currently working toward.

September 23

"God can bring purpose out of pain."

Prompt:

Write about a time you used your own struggle to help someone else.

September 24

"Your daily life is part of your testimony."

Prompt:

Describe a moment from today that you would want to remember a year from now.

SEPTEMBER 25

"God's faithfulness is worth writing down."

Prompt:

Write about a specific prayer God answered in the last year.

SEPTEMBER 26

"Your words can leave a legacy."

Prompt:

Write about a piece of advice you hope people remember you for.

SEPTEMBER 27

"God's peace can come in unexpected ways."

Prompt:

Write about a time you felt calm in the middle of a stressful situation.

SEPTEMBER 28

"Your story can encourage others to take a leap of faith."

Prompt:

Write about a time you stepped into the unknown and what happened.

SEPTEMBER 29

"God can turn interruptions into blessings."

Prompt:

Write about a time your plans changed suddenly but led to something good.

SEPTEMBER 30

"You've completed nine months. Your story is growing stronger every day."

Prompt:

Write about the biggest change you've seen in yourself since starting this journey.

SEPTEMBER – STEADY PROGRESS

End-of-Month Reflection

- How many days did you write this month?
- Which prompt flowed most naturally for you?
- Did you share any of your writing this month? What was the response?
- How often did writing feel therapeutic?
- What's one thing you want to remember from this month's writing?

New Month Intention *(October)*

- Word or theme for the next month: _____
- One personal story I want to finally put into words: _____
- How many days will I commit to writing? _____
- A person I want to write to or about: _____
- I hope my writing this month will help me feel: _____

October

hope*writers

OCTOBER 1

"God's mercies don't fade with the seasons."

Prompt:

Write about one thing you want to focus on this month and why it matters to you right now.

OCTOBER 2

"Your story can bring comfort to someone else's heart."

Prompt:

Write about a time you encouraged someone who was grieving or hurting. Describe what you said or did.

OCTOBER 3

"Sometimes the smallest details remind us of the greatest truths."

Prompt:

Describe a small but meaningful moment from today in vivid detail.

OCTOBER 4

"Even storms have lessons to teach us."

Prompt:

Write about a literal storm you've experienced (what it looked, sounded, and felt like) and any spiritual lesson it brought to mind.

OCTOBER 5

"God uses people to reflect His love."

Prompt:

Write about a person who showed you love in a way you didn't expect.

OCTOBER 6

"Your words can breathe life into weary souls."

Prompt:

Write a note of encouragement to someone you know who's facing a challenge right now.

OCTOBER 7

"God's timing is always perfect, even when it feels late."

Prompt:

Write about something you thought you had missed out on, but God brought it back in His time.

October 8

"Your story is part of God's bigger plan."

Prompt:

Write about a time you realized your actions were part of something much larger than you thought.

OCTOBER 9

"God meets us in the ordinary moments."

Prompt:

Describe a simple daily ritual that helps you feel grounded.

OCTOBER 10

"Friendships can stretch us in ways we don't expect."

Prompt:

Write about a friendship that helped you grow.

OCTOBER 11

"God can bring light in the middle of darkness."

Prompt:

Write about a time you felt hopeless but experienced a breakthrough.

OCTOBER 12

"Your story might be someone else's turning point."

Prompt:

Write about a time you shared something personal and it encouraged another person to take action.

October 13

"God's creation speaks to our hearts."

Prompt:

Describe an autumn scene—colors, smells, sounds—and how it makes you feel.

OCTOBER 14

"Big changes often begin with quiet first steps."

Prompt:

Write about something in your life that started small but became meaningful over time.

हope✷writers

OCTOBER 15

"God uses people to shape our lives."

Prompt:

Write about a mentor, teacher, or leader who left a lasting impact on you.

October 16

"The right words can help mend what's been broken."

Prompt:

Write about a conversation that helped restore a broken relationship.

October 17

"God is with you in every season of change."

Prompt:

Write about a recent change in your life and how you've seen God in it.

OCTOBER 18

"Your perspective can shift the story."

Prompt:

Write about a situation where you chose to see the good instead of focusing on the bad.

OCTOBER 19

"God's blessings often come through the hands of others."

Prompt:

Write about a time someone met a need you had before you even asked.

OCTOBER 20

"Your life is full of stories worth remembering."

Prompt:

Write about a moment from your teenage years that shaped who you are today.

OCTOBER 21

"God's grace can rewrite your story."

Prompt:

Write about a time you experienced grace when you didn't deserve it.

OCTOBER 22

"Your story is still unfolding."

Prompt:

Write about something you hope to accomplish before the end of the year.

OCTOBER 23

"God can bring beauty from ashes."

Prompt:

Write about a loss or disappointment that eventually led to something good.

OCTOBER 24

"Your everyday life can inspire others."

Prompt:

Describe something ordinary you did today in a way that would make it interesting for a reader.

OCTOBER 25

"Writing helps us hold on to the things that matter most."

Prompt:

Write about a time God provided for you in a way that surprised you.

OCTOBER 26

"Your words can live on after you."

Prompt:

Write about a piece of advice or encouragement you hope will be remembered after you're gone.

hope*writers

OCTOBER 27

"God's peace can reach you anywhere."

Prompt:

Write about a place where you feel calm and safe—and why.

OCTOBER 28

"Your story can inspire others to take a step of faith."

Prompt:

Write about a time you said "yes" to something you felt God was asking you to do.

OCTOBER 29

"Sometimes the detours end up leading us somewhere good."

Prompt:

Write about a time an unexpected change of plans worked out for the better.

OCTOBER 30

"Your life is a living testimony."

Prompt:

Write about a decision you made because of your faith.

October 31

"You've completed ten months. Your words are building a lasting legacy."

Prompt:

Write about one way your writing has deepened your faith this year.

October – Courage & Clarity

End-of-Month Reflection

- How many days did you write this month?
- Which prompt required the most courage?
- Did you write anything you feel ready to share publicly?
- Has your sense of your own voice grown clearer?
- What is one area of life you're seeing differently because of writing?

New Month Intention *(November)*

- Word or theme for the next month: _____
- One difficult topic I want to approach with grace: _____
- How many days will I commit to writing? _____
- One way I will share encouragement this month: _____
- I hope my writing this month will bring peace to: _____

November

hope*writers

NOVEMBER 1

"God's mercies are fresh every day—and so are your opportunities to write."

Prompt:

Write about one goal you want to focus on this month and why it matters to you.

NOVEMBER 2

"Your story can be a lifeline for someone else."

Prompt:

Write about a time you shared an experience that made someone feel less alone.

NOVEMBER 3

"God works in the little things as well as the big."

Prompt:

Describe a small blessing from today that lifted your spirits.

NOVEMBER 4

"Even challenges can grow our faith."

Prompt:

Write about a recent challenge and what you learned through it.

November 5

"God uses people to remind us of His love."

Prompt:

Write about a time someone encouraged you when you needed it most.

NOVEMBER 6

"Your words can strengthen someone's faith."

Prompt:

Write a note to a friend, telling them one way you've seen God work in their life.

NOVEMBER 7

"Not everything happens on our schedule."

Prompt:

Write about something you prayed for that happened later than you wanted—but at the perfect time.

NOVEMBER 8

"Your story is part of a bigger picture."

Prompt:

Write about a time you realized God was using your life to impact others.

NOVEMBER 9

"God is present in your daily rhythms."

Prompt:

Describe one part of your morning routine and why it's important to you.

NOVEMBER 10

"Your relationships are a reflection of God's care."

Prompt:

Write about a friend who has been faithful through the ups and downs of life.

NOVEMBER 11

"God can bring peace in the middle of uncertainty."

Prompt:

Write about a time you felt calm despite not knowing how things would turn out.

NOVEMBER 12

"Your story might be the encouragement someone needs today."

Prompt:

Write about a time you told a personal story that gave someone hope.

NOVEMBER 13

"God's creation points us back to Him."

Prompt:

Describe a moment outside—maybe in the crisp air of fall—that made you feel grateful.

NOVEMBER 14

"Small steps can lead to big change."

Prompt:

Write about one habit or change you made that has improved your life.

NOVEMBER 15

"God shapes us through the people He places in our path."

Prompt:

Write about a person who taught you a lesson you still remember today.

NOVEMBER 16

"Your words can heal broken relationships."

Prompt:

Write about a conversation that helped you reconcile with someone.

NOVEMBER 17

"God is with you in every transition."

Prompt:

Write about a time you entered a new season of life and how you adapted.

NOVEMBER 18

"Your perspective can change the way you tell your story."

Prompt:

Write about a situation you see differently now than when it happened.

NOVEMBER 19

"God's blessings often come through others."

Prompt:

Write about a time someone gave you exactly what you needed, even without you asking.

NOVEMBER 20

"Your life is filled with moments worth remembering."

Prompt:

Write about a favorite holiday tradition and where it started.

NOVEMBER 21

"God's grace is greater than your mistakes."

Prompt:

Write about a time you made a poor choice and still experienced grace.

NOVEMBER 22

"You're still becoming the person you're meant to be."

Prompt:

Write about something you're anticipating in the near future and how you're preparing for it.

NOVEMBER 23

"God can bring beauty from disappointment."

Prompt:

Write about a setback that later led to something better.

NOVEMBER 24

"Your everyday life holds extraordinary moments."

Prompt:

Describe a moment from this week that you don't want to forget.

NOVEMBER 25

"God's faithfulness is worth documenting."

Prompt:

Write about a time God answered a prayer in an unexpected way.

NOVEMBER 26

"Your words can live beyond you."

Prompt:

Write about a story, quote, or piece of advice from someone who has passed away that still impacts you.

November 27

"Where we are often shapes how we feel."

Prompt:

Write about your "happy place" and why it matters to you.

NOVEMBER 28

"When we write honestly, we show others they're not alone."

Prompt:

Write about a time you took a risk and what came from it.

NOVEMBER 29

"God can turn delays into blessings."

Prompt:

Write about a time you were frustrated by a delay—and later saw why it was necessary.

NOVEMBER 30

"You've completed eleven months. The finish line is in sight."

Prompt:

Write about the biggest personal or spiritual change you've noticed since starting this writing journey.

November – Gratitude & Grounding

End-of-Month Reflection

- How many days did you write this month?
- Which prompt reminded you to be most grateful?
- Did writing help you process any difficult emotions?
- What's one moment from this month you'll treasure?
- How connected do you feel to your writing purpose right now (1–10)?

New Month Intention *(December)*

- Word or theme for the next month: _____
- One story I want to capture before the year ends: _____
- How many days will I commit to writing? _____
- One way I want to celebrate my writing progress: _____
- I hope my writing this month will prepare me for: _____

December

hope*writers

hope*writers

DECEMBER 1

"God's mercies are new even as the year draws to a close."

Prompt:

Write about one thing you want to finish before the year ends—and why.

DECEMBER 2

"Your story can be the encouragement someone needs this season."

Prompt:

Write about a time you brightened someone's day during the holidays.

DECEMBER 3

"God works in small, quiet ways."

Prompt:

Describe a small act of kindness you noticed this week.

December 4

"Even in the busiest seasons, God is near."

Prompt:

Write about a moment of peace you've experienced in the middle of a hectic time.

DECEMBER 5

"Moments of care remind us we're not alone."

Prompt:

Write about someone who made you feel cared for this year.

DECEMBER 6

"Your words can help someone carry their burden."

Prompt:
Write a short prayer or note of encouragement for a friend going through a difficult time.

December 7

"God's timing is perfect, even in delays."

Prompt:

Write about a time you had to wait longer than you wanted and what came from that waiting.

December 8

"The choices you make often ripple into the lives of others."

Prompt:

Write about one way you've seen your life connect with someone else's this year.

December 9

"God is present in everyday life."

Prompt:

Describe a moment from this week that reminded you of His presence.

DECEMBER 10

"Every relationship leaves an imprint on us."

Prompt:

Write about a friendship that has been a blessing to you this year.

DECEMBER 11

"God can bring light in dark seasons."

Prompt:

Write about a time you felt discouraged this year and how you found hope again.

DECEMBER 12

"Your story can help someone see what's possible."

Prompt:

Write about a personal goal you achieved this year and how you made it happen.

DECEMBER 13

"God's creation is a reminder of His beauty."

Prompt:

Describe a winter scene—real or imagined—that makes you feel at peace.

DECEMBER 14

"Small beginnings can grow into something lasting."

Prompt:

Write about something you started this year that you hope to continue.

DECEMBER 15

"God shapes us through the people we meet."

Prompt:

Write about someone you met this year who impacted you in a meaningful way.

December 16

"Your words can mend relationships."

Prompt:

Write about a conversation you had this year that brought reconciliation.

DECEMBER 17

"Transitions shape us, even when we don't feel ready for them."

Prompt:

Write about a big change that happened this year and what it taught you.

DECEMBER 18

"Your perspective can change everything."

Prompt:

Write about a situation from this year that you now see differently than you did in the moment.

DECEMBER 19

"Some of life's greatest gifts come from the people around us."

Prompt:

Write about a time someone went out of their way to help you this year.

DECEMBER 20

"Your life is full of moments worth remembering."

Prompt:

Write about your favorite memory from this year so far.

DECEMBER 21

"God's grace is always enough."

Prompt:

Write about a time you fell short but experienced His grace.

DECEMBER 22

"Your future holds stories you haven't lived yet."

Prompt:

Write about a dream you have for the coming year.

DECEMBER 23

"Out of challenges, new possibilities can emerge."

Prompt:

Write about a disappointment from this year that led to something unexpectedly good.

DECEMBER 24

"God often speaks in the stillness."

Prompt:

Describe a quiet Christmas Eve or holiday moment that stands out in your memory.

DECEMBER 25

"For unto us a child is born."

Prompt:

Write about your favorite Christmas tradition and what it means to you.

DECEMBER 26

"Looking back helps us see how far we've come."

Prompt:

Recall a memory that continues to give you strength today.

DECEMBER 27

"What you share can continue to influence others long after."

Prompt:

Write about a story or piece of advice you want to pass down to future generations.

DECEMBER 28

"God's peace can meet you anywhere."

Prompt:

Write about a moment this year when you felt completely at peace.

DECEMBER 29

"Your story can inspire others to take action."

Prompt:

Write about a time this year when you stepped out in faith.

December 30

"God can turn endings into beginnings."

Prompt:

Write about an ending you experienced this year and the new thing that came after.

hope*writers

DECEMBER 31

"You've completed a year of writing—and your story is stronger than ever."

Prompt:

Look back over your year of writing and choose three entries you're most proud of. Write about why they matter to you.

December – Reflection & Renewal

End-of-Month Reflection

- How many days did you write this month?
- Looking back over the year, what's your proudest writing moment?
- Which prompt had the most lasting impact on you?
- How has writing changed your perspective since January?
- What's the most surprising thing you discovered about yourself this year?